Model Soldiers

W.Y. Carman

Model Soldiers

Charles Letts and Company Limited

Published by
Charles Letts and Company Limited

Head Office:
Diary House, Borough Road, London, SE1 1DW

Publishing Consultant: Lionel Leventhal

Designed by: Kenneth Farnhill

Photographs: Michael Dyer Associates Limited

First Published 1973
Standard Book Number: 85097 072 5
Text © W. Y. Carman
Illustrations © Charles Letts and Company Limited 1972
The collective work © Charles Letts and Company Limited 1972

Set in 'Monophoto' Times Roman by Cranmer Brown (Filmsetters) Limited
Printed in Great Britain by Colour Reproductions Ltd.,
Billericay, Essex

Contents

Plate	1	The Black Watch, the Royal Highlanders	Fontispiece
		INTRODUCTION	7
Plate	2	Hunting Scene, 1780	16
Plate	3	Three soldiers from Bergmann of Strasbourg	17
Plate	4	Heinrichsen 25 mm tin soldiers	18
Plate	5	Wehrli civilian figures	19
Plates	6–7	Boxed set of tin soldiers from Nuremberg	20–21
Plate	8	Waterloo figures, the Gebrüder Rieche	22
Plate	9	The Royal Scots Greys, 1684–1914	23
Plate	10	Monarchs of Great Britain, Otto Gottstein	24
Plate	11	Assyrian Slave Market, Otto Gottstein	25
Plate	12	Figures from the court of Henry VIII, Otto Gottstein	26
Plate	13	The green at the Tower of London	27
Plate	14	Mignot figures of Napoleon I's period	28
Plate	15	Fritz Mittmann 20 mm figures for dioramas	29
Plate	16	Carved wooden grenadiers and cavalryman	30
Plate	17	Cut-out paper soldiers	31
Plate	18	Cut-out paper soldiers of the *Imprimerie Alsacienne*	32
Plate	19	Toy soldiers of different raw materials	32
Plate	20	Porcelain soldiers of Napoleon's army	34
Plate	21	Japanese lead naval vessels	34
Plate	22	Waterloo figures from model by Siborne	36
Plate	23	Semi-solid figures from Allgeyer of Fürth	37
Plate	24	Allgeyer figures	38
Plate	25	Figures by Elastolin of Neustadt	39
Plate	26	Elastolin and Lineol figures of the Nazi era	40
Plate	27	Early Britains' cavalry	41
Plate	28	Britains' figures with improved details	42
Plate	29	Collection of Britains' hussars	42
Plate	30	Britains' lancers	44
Plate	31	Britains' figures including Boer soldiers	45
Plate	32	Britains' Highlanders and unidentified penny figures	46
Plate	33	Britains' Royal Welsh Fusiliers; goat major, J. Hill Co.	47
Plate	34	Britains' Royal Horse Artillery; Carman officer	48

Plate 35	Britains' Royal Field Artillery and Marines; Carman officer	49
Plate 36	Britains' mountain artillery	50
Plate 37	Britains' Royal Engineers	51
Plate 38	Britains' Medical Services	52
Plate 39	Britains' Army Service Corps wagon and limbered wagon	53
Plate 40	Britains' Naval Figures	54
Plate 41	Britains' Royal Marines and Marines Band	55
Plate 42	Royal Air Force figures, Britains and John Hill Company	56
Plate 43	Indian figures, Britains, Mignot, Rose Models, Authenticast	57
Plates 44–45	African figures, Britains, Mignot and others	58–59
Plates 46–47	Britains' 'B' and 45 mm soldiers	60–61
Plates 48–49	Large-scale figures, Britains, Johillco and others	62–63
Plates 50–51	Plastic figures from continental countries	64–65
Plate 52	Aluminium figures	66
Plate 53	Heyde figures	67
Plate 54	Smaller Heyde figures	68
Plate 55	Courtenay and Doran medieval figures	69
Plate 56	Britains' Medieval figures	70
Plate 57	Other historical figures	71
Plate 58	Royal figures, Courtenay; military figures, Carman	72
Plate 59	Holger Eriksson figures	73
Plate 60	Figures from makers in different countries	74
Plate 61	Figures of the French of Napoleon's time	75
Plate 62	The British at Waterloo	76
Plate 63	Model of the Colour Court, St. James's Palace	77
Plate 64	Soldiers by Greenwood, Nicholson and Niblett	78
Plate 65	'Willie' figures by Edward Suren	79
	SELECT BIBLIOGRAPHY	80
	SELECTED MUSEUMS WHERE DISPLAYS MAY BE SEEN	80

Model Soldiers

INTRODUCTION

The origins of the model soldier may be traced back to prehistoric times. One may, for example, see plaster and wood models of Ancient-Egyptian spearmen who were made to guard a noble of the Middle Kingdom in his tomb. In Cyprus and elsewhere one may see crude pottery figurines both of foot soldiers and cavalrymen made in the fifth century before Christ. There are leaden castings of Greek and Roman warriors which might have been votive figures but they might have been household possessions as well.

In the Middle Ages there is no doubt that small jousting knights were used as toys and it may be that many miniature soldiers have disappeared without trace. This was also the fate of the large silver armies made for rich kings and princes in the early-eighteenth century because the very value of the metal ensured the destruction of these toy soldiers. By the end of the eighteenth century the men who were making dolls' furniture and household items were thinking about pewter figures of soldiers and animals. The flat tin-mixture articles could be produced cheaply enough in quantity to be toys. The examples which remain in continental museums illustrate a wide variety of types and engravers. The true extent of the craft may never be known. A pewterer would fill in his spare time making these toys to be sold by weight leaving other enterprising vendors to undertake the painting, if any, and resale to customers with sufficient money.

The paper or the wooden soldier could also be produced in quantity to be within the reach of the poorer child. These of course were even more perishable than the tin or lead soldier. However the industrial expansion of the nineteenth and twentieth centuries brought forth a great variety of the toy and model soldier, many of which are antiques by age and valuable by rarity as well as being artistic and beautiful in design. Today the rise in the cost of certain metals has taken the tin and lead soldier away from the toy class. The advent of 'plastic' has filled the deficiency and produced a figure so cheap that it has speeded up the demise of the metal toy. Unfortunately in many cases the results are of such poor workmanship that many collectors tend to overlook them. This means that the collector who is discriminating generally confines his collection to the more expensive figures if he wishes to maintain a high standard.

Although there may be some toy soldiers in museums, many collections are in private hands, having been preserved in the family—often only by accident. As most model soldiers were originally intended to be toys, and, as such, were frequently passed from generation to generation of children, there have, perforce, been many casualties, resulting in the loss of whole sets of the older figures. On the other hand, in households where discipline has been enforced, the toy soldiers may still be immured in their original boxes in a cupboard or trunk. In the past, when they were discovered, they were preserved simply because of sentimental attachment, thus providing modern collectors with beautifully-kept sets of old figures. Nowadays the financial aspect is a considerable incentive to the collector, but until a few years ago, the male adult was satisfied to use the toy soldiers to recreate a parade, an incident or a battlescene, and it was with such men that the British Society of Collectors of Model Soldiers began, thus becoming the oldest society of model-soldier collectors in the English-speaking world. The title changed later to the British Model Soldier Society when the activities of the society expanded.

Today a beginner does not have to rely on accidentally-preserved toys but he or she can begin with modern productions of a high standard never dreamed of some thirty years ago. In the past there was little information and few skills available to aid and improve a collection. Today, however, any subject in history may be reproduced with the wide technological knowledge at hand. And, as for the war-game, there are about as many societies for this branch as there were original members of the British Model Soldier Society. This book does not propose to include details of the war-game, but H. G. Wells's books *Floor Games* and *Little Wars* (see Bibliography) will provide the reader with a good introduction to this subject.

The range of collectable model and toy soldiers is considerable. The most prolific and frequently the most artistic field is that of the tin soldier, although most collections of these are to be found on the Continent. By 1780 special figures like that of Frederick the Great of Prussia (based on a well-known portrait), Greek gods and goddesses and contemporary cavalrymen were made in a most artistic style. These figures, cast in a mixture of tin and lead could achieve the smallest detail that could be engraved in the slate mould. Pure tin is not used on its own as the metal is too hard and brittle. Lead, on the other hand, is too soft and does not take the detail of a mould; but a mixture of both metals produces a semi-flexible soldier with much detail.

Many manufacturers in Europe made figures throughout the Napoleonic wars but their models are rare and to be seen mainly in museums. It was through the firm of Heinrichsen of Nuremberg, which worked so long and so prolifically to satisfy children and indeed older persons, that the cult of the tin soldier established itself so strongly. The tin soldier referred to by Hans Christian Andersen is this type of toy. Tin soldiers of 40 mm scale were also made popular by the Gebrüder Rieche of Hanover who continued production well into the twentieth century. But it was the small 25 mm figures that reached the widest market not only in Germany but overseas. When the engraver Ludwig Frank joined the firm of Heinrichsen in this century his craftsmanship improved the declining standards and he established the 30 mm scale which is now practically standard among the private editors. Frank later engraved moulds for Ochel of Kiel and continued the high artistic qualities that took the tin figure out of the toy category.

The keenness of the German collectors to find figures for periods other than those in the commercial fields led many to finance their own special moulds. Thus becoming private editors, they created special tin figures to exchange with other collectors. O. E. Gottstein of Leipzig and Paul Armont of Paris were two such men who were in the forefront of financing figures as a hobby. Other German collectors followed and even today there are many private collectors producing tin figures from the ancient world right up to the modern battles, plus those for many historical events.

The cost of tin was always relatively high, and thus the tin soldier was expensive, but today the tin figure is removed entirely from the toy category because of its cost. The acquisition of those flat, metal figures is still, however, a very desirable pursuit for adult collectors. As these models are flat and mainly in silhouette, they do not have the realism of a three-dimensional figure. Collecting them is, thus, a more specialist taste and flourishes strongly on the Continent. There the tin soldier, set in a diorama or model setting, may be seen in many museums.

A toy soldier made out of tin in the eighteenth century would have been the toy of a middle-class child but the soldier cut out of a paper sheet would have also been within the reach of a poor man's child. Thus these paper warriors were once very popular throughout Europe. The crudely coloured woodcuts of the seventeenth and eighteenth centuries came from cities like Augsburg, Nuremberg and Leipzig. Eventually Strasbourg established itself as a leader and home of the paper soldier. The thin printed sheets, with several figures on each, were stuck on thin but stiff card. Then the soldiers were cut out with a sharp knife or scissors. A small block of wood or a folded triangle of card made the support to keep the soldier upright.

England also produced soldier-sheets in the Napoleonic era, perhaps as an extension of the toy theatre, although the known sheets have no relation to any play. Many cut-out figures of Napoleon's army exist, produced by hand and not from any published engraving. Cheap lithography brought coloured sheets within the reach of everyone. The fragility of paper did not tend towards preservation and most examples must have perished long ago. Heightened with gold and silver, other military sheets were preserved for their artistic value. Later cheap sheets have a basic figure in colour with others left in black and white for the owner to colour. These sheets were usually stuck on stout card by the purchaser but later soldiers were printed directly on to stiff card and partly cut out by machinery to produce military 'scraps'. These when pressed out could be mounted on small blocks so that the soldiers stood upright.

The First World War saw the appearance of large coloured sheets printed on both sides. These were so carefully printed that when cut out the soldiers or groups were perfect both front and back. Colour supplements in newspapers also had the combatants, about five inches high, intended to be pasted on thin card and to be cut out by hand. These fragile soldiers could not have lasted many months. Cut-out books were also produced in England at the time of great events like coronations. Commercial packaging also was a place for these card soldiers. The tradition of the toy soldier on sheets of paper still continues in such countries as France, Italy, Spain and even one iron-curtain country, Poland.

Carved wooden toys were produced in the earliest days by peasants in forest areas. These carved figures may have at first been intended for personal use but they were later made commercially, and are still made today in parts of Germany. The native warrior of East Africa and his uniformed successor were locally carved in the Second World War and may be available today. One type of mass-produced wooden figure was the 'Dutch-doll' version. This stiff figure with its jointed arms and legs had its militant counterparts—the sailors and 'Indians' in their distinctive wooden boats—before the First World War. The wooden grenadiers in red coats, white trousers and black bearskin were created by a different process. They were turned on a lathe, the surplus parts being cut down and arms, rifles and stands being glued on later. These may still be bought today, packed in chipwood boxes resting on a bed of wood shavings.

The tin soldier was a comparatively easy figure to produce by a pewterer who had the metal and techniques right at hand. Unfortunately it was not a very lucrative employment and often bulk tin soldiers were made as a spare time occupation. The increasing cost of tin led to experiments with other materials. A figure completely made of lead would be cheaper but too soft, too heavy and with poor detail. The addition of weapons could not be achieved by ordinary soldering methods. Thus a new 'composition' figure came into being. This mixture may have included lead, some tin, antimony and even zinc. The makers of tin soldiers discovered that they could adapt slate moulds to take the new metal. The same height could be kept but the figure had to be thicker so that the metal flowed properly. Thus the semi-round figure came on to the market in the second half of the nineteenth century. J. C. Allgeyer, the nineteenth-century maker in Fürth, produced natives in both flat 'tin' and half-rounded 'lead'. These new toys were stronger than the tin soldier and had considerable new features, including separate rider and horse. Three-dimensional cannon and vehicles produced a more natural overall appearance which has not dated, for some have been used in modern war-games.

As the new mixture became extensively used larger figures came into production. Some readers may recollect the aluminium moulds marked 'GMBH' which were sold before 1939 and were often used by Boy Scouts making model soldiers to sell to raise funds. With these moulds enthusiasts were able to make their own figures, supplying their own raw materials. The results were, therefore, often very rough and crude.

The 40 mm Heyde cavalry figures show that they originate from these flat-surfaced moulds because the flattened riders had arms which bent forward and sword scabbards which bent backwards. The horse with all four feet on a narrow stand had its artistic limitations. Heyde also produced larger figures fully round and with much detail. Trade competition caused these expensive lines to be discontinued in favour of the smaller figures which could be bent into many positions and varied by different plug-in heads. Lucotte figures with added parts also had to give way to the simple Mignot solid 50 mm soldier with the minimum of added detail.

The solid German soldiers held the British market in late-Victorian times.

Heyde civilians and 'beef-eaters' are illustrated in H. G. Wells's *Floor Games*. About 1890 the firm of William Britain produced his hollow-cast soldiers, which were of a desirable size, lightness for handling and cheapness. The 'lead' was, of course, a mixture. The ingenious metal moulds were made of two or more pieces which hinged together to make a 'box' to hold the molten metal. A quick movement poured out the excess metal from the interior before all had chilled to the mould. The weight of the metal pressed the shell of the figure fully into the engraved details.

Britains' first soldiers had fixed arms. The swords of the cavalry were not lead, but strips of thin tin-plate cast into the horse. By 1896 the cavalry figures had a moveable arm, an extra production process, but one which eliminated the complicated tin sword. The first lancers also had a short and solid lance fixed to the soldier, but, by 1903, the lance arm was separate and moveable with a metal rod for the lance. The first infantrymen also had fixed arms. One method of adding the awkward rifle was to plug in a separate piece at the right cuff. The moveable arm for infantry came in 1897. Band instruments were at first on slotted and fixed arms but, by 1911, the arms had become moveable. Most original oval stands of infantry were replaced by oblong ones by 1906.

Britains also made smaller soldiers, British and foreign, of the 45 mm scale. These appeared about 1899 and, strangely enough, were still in the catalogue just before the Second World War. The fascinating Royal Horse Artillery gun team at the gallop, in full dress and in service dress, was also listed in later years.

The artillery of the tin soldier in the mid-nineteenth century often included a cannon which fired a small dried pea or a piece of wood. The hollow tin-metal gun-barrel contained an internal coiled spring of thin wire which, having been compressed by a wire pulled through the breech end, had sufficient strength when released to propel the ammunition. Messrs. Britains developed their own cannon with special firing mechanism. One popular method was to use a stout metal lever set in the trail, which was actuated by a flat metal piece of the clock-spring variety. When the lever was released upwards, it entered a slot in the cannon barrel and hit the end of a short piece of metal rod which served as the ammunition. This flew a considerable distance and knocked the lead soldier down if a direct hit was scored. A later refinement was the addition of an explosive cap as used in a toy pistol. This cap was placed on a circular spot at the breech of the gun. When the lever was knocked up, it hit the cap at the same time as the metal rod and made a suitable explosion. This was an attractive feature for small boys who wished to see positive action but the bane of many a future collector who found headless and dented soldiers in the old collections.

The advent of the Boer War and the Russo-Japanese War brought toy soldiers of the opposing forces on to the market. In 1908 Britains published a colourful booklet, *The Great War Game for Young and Old,* which combined photographs of actual soldiers with those of the lead figures. H. G. Wells, perhaps inspired by this work, wrote his *Floor Games* in 1911. His *Little Wars* first appeared in the Windsor Magazine of December 1912 and January 1913, the complete book coming out in the latter year. H. G. Wells used his *Little Wars* to demonstrate the futility of war. By the time of the First World War not only were Britains producing khaki warriors but several new firms were successfully marketing their own figures although at times cases of copyright breaking occurred.

The coronation of King George VI in 1936 was marked by the appearance of a good model of the golden State Coach with the King and Queen inside. The large display box also had footmen, grooms and Yeomen of the Guard, thus making an imposing and attractive set. It is interesting to note that, in deference to those parents who objected to the warlike nature of toy soldiers, Messrs. Britains began a policy of producing civilian models. These covered not only farm figures but also characters from children's books and films like *Snow White and the Seven Dwarfs*. Railway staff, Salvation Army men and women, Boy Scouts and football teams had existed before the First World War. Now railwaymen were given modern dress and the addition of workmen with shovels was satisfying to the model railway enthusiast. The types of policemen were increased in number but the greatest development took place in the farm and zoological series which covered a wide selection of animals, agricultural appliances and personnel. At the annual British Industries Fairs, a Britains' model village where all aspects of the peaceful country life were shown was often an attractive feature. On one occasion Queen Mary commented that the only lack was that of the village idiot. The next year saw that deficiency filled! The outbreak of the Second World War, however, saw many new soldiers in contemporary uniform, men in gasmasks, fire-fighting garments and even a barrage balloon.

After the war airborne infantry, parachute troops, ski troops and men of the Royal Armoured Corps were added to the lines on sale. Foreign armies now included Danish, Papal and Russian soldiers. The Confederate and Union soldiers of the American Civil War were obviously destined for an American market and new Royal Canadian Mounted Police and the Fort Henry Guards were aimed at another American market.

The hollow soldier was imitated by other British firms but many products were of lower and even poor quality. John Hill Company was one firm which kept a high standard and a very wide range of soldiers, but not being as well documented as Britains it tends to be overlooked. 'Johillco' (one of the company's trade marks) continued to make figures up until recent years. There are many names to be found among the makers of hollow lead soldiers in the reign of King Edward VII. James Renvoise, Hanks, Abel, Reka (or C. W. Baker) are some of the names. Later makers include A. Fry, Taylor and Barrett, Charbens, Timpo, Cherilea, Crescent, Fylde, and Stoddart. Although many soldiers produced by these makers are not of the best standard they are still desirable because of their rarity.

The arrival of plastic material, including alkathene, brought a cheaper toy on to the market. These materials being slightly flexible gave greater freedom of design for dramatic poses and detail. Unfortunately the cheapness of competitive producers frequently lowered the standard in Great Britain although figures in France and Belgium were most artistic. As a toy the plastic soldiers have almost disappeared although complex and expensive figures are still available to the expert.

The name of Robert Courtenay stands out as that of the first British maker of the fighting man as a work of art. His solid castings after the First World War were gems of heraldic painting. Although specialising in 'knights' of the medieval period, he later made special personalities and, following the inspiration of Gottstein, even ventured into Assyrians and Ancient Egyptians. The need for models of the British Army of the past was recognised in 1937 when the British Model Soldier Society decided to match the French Army of Napoleon, in the Royal United Service Museum, with the appropriate British troops. At that time I produced a solid infantryman with separate arms, weapons and pack, on the lines of the figures of Lucotte, the nineteenth-century French manufacturer. Messrs. Britain generously undertook to make two basic figures of infantry and Highlanders which became regular selling lines. I then produced a solid marching infantryman with an attached musket. An Elizabethan footsoldier and English-Civil-War figures of pikemen and musketeers followed. After 1945 I made soldiers of the 45 Rebellion, Magna Carta knights, Henry VIII, Queen Elizabeth I and others for general sale. F. Ping made special individual figures of warriors and personalities and his handicraft may still be found in London. J. A. Greenwood, of Greenwood and Ball, made sand-cast solid figures, animated and soldered to separate bases.

It was the advent of the flexible mould that outmoded the two-piece metal mould as well as sand-cast and plaster-mould figures. The new material permitted much detail without expensive die-sinking and even slight undercuts could be tolerated as the mould could spring back into position. Graham Farish, already established in model railways, developed a range of figures at the time of the coronation of Queen Elizabeth II, in 1953. The slightly larger figures covered the notable people of the coronation as well as historical figures like Bonnie Prince Charlie, the flamboyant 1830 military fashions and other. Unfortunately this production had a short life although the standard was high.

Norman Newton developed and sold the figures originally designed by Charles Stadden. These figures set a new standard for historical British soldiers. The animation or positioning of the soldier made many variations on the basic figure and helped extend the range. These figures, made with a metal of high tin content, are expensive even as a raw material, and the difficulties in training painters keeps the figures out of the toy class. The firm of Tradition, in Piccadilly, London, not only covers the smaller war-game figure but now supplies a 90 mm soldier, which must definitely be regarded as an ornament.

The flexible mould has brought the art of the model soldier within the reach of many amateurs both in Britain and in the United States of America. Many of these are very good but others are anatomically incorrect and may not be sought after in years to come, although others certainly will be. R. Gammage, of Rose Miniatures, specialises in the 54 mm scale, producing figures in roles which range from the ancient world through the armies of Europe up to the present day—all of good proportion and careful detail. Marcus Hinton, of Hinton Hunt Figures, makes solid historical fighting men with a characteristic ruggedness.

It may be that the 20, 25 and 30 mm solid soldiers became popular either because they were cheaper to buy or because a large collection of these would take up relatively little space, but there is no doubt now that the small figure is most appreciated by the war-gamer, who can assemble and handle sizeable battalions. Before the

1939–45 war Britains' standard and 'W' soldiers made up the war-gamers' armies. The new size allows a battle to be fought on a table in a small room instead of on a large floor. The great variety of historical periods now covered by modern manufacturers has led to the creation of many war-gaming societies—even one for ancient warfare.

The standard of the small soldier varies greatly from the cheapest (and often poorest modelling) to the exquisite details and styling of figures made by Edward Suren of Willie Figures (see page 79). Whether all 20-30 mm soldiers will survive to be collectors' pieces is doubtful but it is sure that many will.

J. Niblett, successful as a pattern maker, markets his own range of 20 mm knights and Civil War soldiers, all delicate figures, usually with extra weapons soldered on. Hinton Hunt, Rose Models and Tradition all have the miniature war-game figures usually of one piece. Edward Suren specializes in the 30 mm solid figure which reaches a high degree of perfection. These are more suitable for a diorama or a set piece than to being exposed to possible damage on a battlefield. His Prussian soldiers of 1870 have heavy Germanic plodding attitudes whereas the elegant French officer almost minces into action in his tight-fitting garments. When set out in a model with buildings or trees, the figures look most realistic and when photographed may be enlarged without losing their detail. Special details are not forgotten, as in the battle of Omdurman where the mounted figure of Winston Churchill smoked a recognisable cigar.

All the miniature soldiers which are in production today are not mentioned in this brief account because this is a guide to toys and model soldiers of the past which might still appear on the antique market or in the salerooms. On the Continent certain museums may be able to show collections and supply information about these small soldiers but such information is scarce in this country. There are museums like the Museum of Childhood in Edinburgh and that in Bethnal Green, London, which are building up collections and it is hoped that, in the not too distant future, good representation and satisfactory documentation will be available to the collector and connoisseur to enable him to study and appraise the particularities which specially interest him.

In the United States of America there are many local societies for collectors of both antique and modern model soldiers. It is, therefore, not possible to include them all here, but, at the time of going to press two of the larger societies, which also both produce their own publications are: Miniature Figure Collectors of America, of which the headquarters are in Ardmore, Pennsylvania, and which publishes *Guidon* quarterly; and, National Capital Military Collectors, with its headquarters in Bethesda, Maryland, which produces the publication *Vedette*.

There are, similarly, many modern makers of connoisseur figures in the United States, of which the following is a list of some of the better-known ones: Imrie/Risley Miniatures, Incorporated of Long Island, New York; Chris Farbre of Drexel Hill, Pennsylvania; Jack Scruby of Visalia, California; Superior Models Incorporated of Claymont, Delaware; Bugle and Guidon of Jackson, Michigan and H-R Products Incorporated of Morton Grove, Illinois.

Jacket illustration: The chariot group, in the top left-hand corner, shows Caractacus, King of the Britons, in the first century A.D., in his scythe-wheeled chariot. This tin figure was produced by Otto Gottstein, c. 1936, and is in the 30 mm scale. (See also pages 24–26.)

The British general officer, in the lower left-hand corner, is in full dress uniform of c. 1812. This miniature is a modern Stadden figure in the 56 mm or 2¼″ scale.

The various scales of the continental tin soldiers and other figures were based on the actual height of the figure, that is, 25, 30 or 40 mm, without taking the headdress into consideration. British-made figures, which were formerly known by their height in inches are now being quoted in millimetres.

Frontispiece: This shows the pipe band and men of the Black Watch, the Royal Highlanders, c. 1910, marching through a gateway and passing a mounted officer. These figures were converted from hollow-cast soldiers, produced by Britains and other manufacturers, in 1937, as the pipes and drums of this regiment had not been produced commercially at that time.

Plate 2

This hunting scene of 1780 is composed of tin figures from the moulds of Adam Schweizer d.A. of Diessen-Ammersee, who produced commercial toys at the end of the eighteenth century. The stylized huntsmen pursue the boar with boar-spears, the rabbit by musket, the deer by horse and the fox with hounds. Characteristic of this engraver is the fanciful tree with highly coloured birds and squirrel on the trunk.

Plate 3

The engravers and editors of the early-nineteenth century produced tin soldiers and figures of many sizes. The three figures on the left are 55 mm high, from Bergmann of Strasbourg about 1831, showing the French uniforms of the period. The maker of the 65 mm jaeger (or hunter) in striped breeches is not known. In the centre is the large 13 cm piece (of 10 cm scale) engraved by H. Hoy. This shows Frederick VII, King of Denmark, in *Livgarden til Hest* uniform, with aluminium helmet c. 1850. The marching Bavarians (50 mm high) are in infantry uniform of 1830.

Plate 4

It was Ernst Heinrichsen, 1806–1888, of Nuremberg, who produced the 25 mm tin soldiers in such quantities that their popularity lasted over a hundred years. The Second World War saw the ancient firm slowing down and only a few soldiers were produced after that conflict. The illustration shows the British uniforms of 1820. The elegant soldiers rest in the camp while cavalry musicians beguile them.

Plate 5

Rudolf Wehrli, 1801–1876, after an apprenticeship in Bavaria, returned to Aarau, in Switzerland, where he produced many figures of the 1830 period. Some 3,000 of his moulds are still preserved in Zurich and many show the influence of Heinrichsen. The civilian figures of the promenade and the market-keepers which had been so popular in Germany and Russia were now to be found in Switzerland.

Plate 6

Tin soldiers were often sold in oval boxes of chipwood, resting on a bed of fine shavings. The tin-soldier makers of Nuremberg, to capture a wider market, produced large set-pieces in boxes covered with shiny green paper and gilt paper strips. The box lid in this picture has a spirited scene of the French Revolution of

Plate 7

1848 depicting the civilians fighting the troops at the barricades. The animated tin figures show the armed women dashing forward to support the tradesmen like the butcher, and the students. Little boys hurl paving-stones at the red-trousered infantry, while people in the houses throw down other missiles.

Plate 8

The Gebrüder Rieche, of Hanover, began making figures of the 30–36 mm sizes in 1806, and later produced famous personages of Waterloo. The wounded Marshal Bessieres in the centre is painted with the care of a miniaturist. The British infantry and the dashing Danish hussar are of the 36 mm scale. The Turkish figures on the left and the Russians on the right come from a special box named the 'Russen u. Türken-Schlacht'. The two large 60 mm Highlanders are from a special order, made by Ochel of Kiel, Germany, for a Parisian collector, to be presented to a British general.

Plate 9

Almost any military incident or regiment throughout history may be portrayed in the modern tin soldier, for there are many hundreds of thousands of figures available. Here a selected regiment, the Royal Scots Greys, is shown from 1684 up to the First World War. These examples of pre-war manufacturers cover Krunert of Austria, Mignot of Paris, Schirmer of Hanover and Ochel of Kiel. Only the Beibel soldier of Waterloo was originally intended for a Scots Grey, the others being converted from French and Austrian cavalrymen.

Plate 10

Otto Gottstein came to England to avoid Nazi pressures, and, as a tribute to his new home, he produced a set of 42 Kings and Queens of Great Britain, ranging from William the Conqueror to George VI. These 30 mm tin figures, engraved by L. Frank, were based on contemporary pictures and the best available evidence. This selection includes William I, Matilda, Richard I, John, Richard III, Edward III, Henry VIII, Elizabeth I, Charles I, Anne, George IV, Victoria, Edward VII, George V, Edward VIII and George VI.

Plate 11

The flat figure lends itself to dioramas and models. This Assyrian slave market of 600 B.C. shows buyers from many lands looking at beautiful women. The scribe notes down the transactions and behind him is a series of weights, fashioned like lions, to assess the payment. The Assyrian King, Assurbanipal, in his chariot follows his bodyguard. These 30 mm figures are from Gottstein moulds and are painted in poster paints not the usual oil.

Plate 12

The life of Henry VIII and his court inspired Gottstein to produce thirty figures mainly based on the famous Holbein pictures and bas-reliefs. The King is surrounded by courtiers including many well-known figures. Cardinal Wolsey may be easily recognised, and Hans Holbein himself sketches those present. The executioner was not in the Gottstein series but was made privately later.

Plate 13

This model shows the green in the Tower of London, near where the executions took place. Here is a more peaceful scene, a review of the Foot Guards of Charles I's reign. These modern 30 mm tin soldiers of Austrian, French and German make are painted as the predecessors of the Grenadier Guards.

Plate 14

The Parisian firm of Mignot (C.B.G.), which normally made lead composition figures, began to produce tin figures in the early thirties. Designed by Rousselot and others, and engraved by Ochel of Kiel, these detailed 30 mm figures show a bivouac of Napoleon I's period. The *vivandière* with her wagon brings extra delicacies for the dragoons and guards. Other refreshments are also being brought but one small boy only brings his wooden horse with Napoleon astride. The 'pips' on the cards of the gambling soldiers may be seen with a magnifying glass. One soldier peels potatoes and a hussar of the Imperial Guard breaks wood to keep the fire alight.

Plate 15

The making of models and small dioramas for the drawing room blossomed into large reconstructions of battlefields for museums and exhibitions. The creation of 20 mm and 15 mm figures enabled many more soldiers to be pressed into the limited space and gave an impression of perspective. In 1930 Fritz Mittmann, 1901–1959, of Schweidnitz, produced the 20 mm soldiers for Waterloo. Other German battles followed later. The smallest commercial figures appear to be 8 mm-high gun crew firing a gun, all in third dimension instead of the flat silhouette of the tin figure. Small figures are now extremely popular for war-games and can be mounted, several together, on one moveable base.

Plate 16

Wooden carved toys have an ancient lineage going back to the beginnings of history. Obviously a peasant father could carve a variety of animals and figures for his children. In the well-wooded areas of the Black Forest, Saxony and Thuringia the tradition is continued today. The red-coated grenadiers of all sizes could not be dated before the mid-nineteenth century because of the tunic, but they are still being produced today, even in chipwood boxes. The cavalryman of Frederick the Great's time is a more sophisticated article and rocks on a wire spring.

Plate 17

Soldiers cut out of paper were also within reach of the poor child. Strasbourg is famed for its paper soldiers, which appeared there before 1740. The popularity of the toy theatre in England brought cut-out sheets for the play of the 'Battle of Waterloo'. The sheets by Redington and Skelton followed the tradition of Pollock's Toy Theatre.

By 1845, the French were producing military sheets in full colour from Silbermann. Late-Victorian sheets were varied but in crude zincotype colours. Partly-embossed and partly-cut-out sheets provided a colourful card army. In modern times cut-outs are published at coronations. Special hand-painted figures like the Highland officer by Colonel O. McLeod appear but rarely.

Plate 18

The tradition of the paper soldier in Alsace brought about a higher standard than those usually seen in Germany. The *Imprimerie Alsacienne* of Gustav Fischbach, successor to Silbermann, made the sheet illustrated. This is number six of a series of ten covering the French Army. Poland, Italy, Portugal and Spain still publish large military cut-out sheets but the quality varies as the market aimed at is usually that of children.

Plate 19

Many raw materials have been used for toy soldiers and substances range from the commonest clay to the best bronze and silver. The crude clay figures of the Chinese Revolutionary Army produced in 1937 contrast with the elaborate Chinese warlord on his caparisoned horse. The unpainted pipeclay of a French zouave shows delicate modelling. The German raw recruit of the late-nineteenth century is an amusing hollow clay figure. The small porcelain dragoon is but a poor version of the many sizes of Napoleonic soldiers produced by Capedimonte and Meissen factories. The two brass figures on the right are Persian soldiers of town and country, which were once partly painted. The two lancers, officers with the beautifully-modelled horse, do not at once reveal that they are expensive Vienna bronze figures made before the First World War.

33

Plate 20

Porcelain soldiers of Napoleon's army are made in many sizes, this green-clad *Chasseur leger* being nearly seven inches high. The tall figure of the havildar of the Bengal Native Infantry is nine inches in height and made, in India, of fired pottery. Although based on a coloured plate in a history book of 1817, there is no doubt that it was made much later. The askari of the Royal West African Frontier Force is a modern five-inch figure made by Howard F. Willetts. Large model soldiers are gaining popularity as better detail and artistic finish may be achieved.

Plate 21

Although there were occasional break-aways from the silhouette outline of the tin soldier, like the assembling of the cannon and wagons to make three-dimensional models, this group of naval vessels is a special departure. In the Russo-Japanese War of 1905, the Japanese were frequently victorious at sea. These soldered-together pieces of lead sail in a horrific sea of frozen waves.

35

Plate 22

The most famous British model soldiers must include those of Captain William Siborne who created two models of Waterloo. The first model put on exhibition at the Egyptian Hall in 1838 had 8 mm figures. The second model also on view in the same hall in 1844 had 25 mm figures which cost £600 in total. The carefully-modelled soldiers had moveable arms and heads and were in the best tradition of the German pewterer. The unpainted figures of Wellington and Napoleon have been lent by Sir Malcolm Henderson, a descendant of the redoubtable captain.

Plate 23

The tin soldier was not a sturdy toy, as the story by Hans Christian Andersen shows. Thus the semi-solid figures from J. C. Allgeyer of Fürth were not only stronger but cheaper because of the high lead content in the 'feine massive' metal. By the 1870s these figures were flooding Europe.

Here the Life Guards band has an imposing array of musical instruments. Although from the side the horses look solid, from the front the four legs can be seen on one plane. The Foot Guards band has a Germanic appearance combined with a wide range of musical instruments. The arbour, with the drinking officers, is an ingenious construction of flat-cast pieces.

Plate 24

Allgeyer often produced the same figure both in flat tin and semi-solid lead. The artillery teams were carefully soldered together as was the ambulance. The stalwart lancers have the right arms bent forward to give a more natural position, and all sit firmly on their horses by means of a prong. The wide variety of unusual figures like the stretcher party, medical staff and fatigue parties brought realism to the rows of similar infantrymen. The pontoon wagon by Allgeyer has wooden planks as well as a tin pontoon.

Plate 25

Although the sawdust-and-glue figures of Elastolin of Neustadt achieved wide popularity about the beginning of the twentieth century with cowboys and Indians, there was also a wide range of soldiers. Among the pre-1914 soldiers is the marching British infantryman 7 cm scale. The Scottish piper is 10 cm high and the small German soldier is only 4 cm high. Lineol, another German firm, made many German soldiers ranging from Frederick the Great and his Grenadiers up to the Nazi Youth. Although Elastolin went out of business during the Second World War, the firm has made a come-back with hard plastic (alkathene) historical types.

Plate 26

Both Elastolin and Lineol of Dresden, produced portrait figures of the Nazi era. Those on the left are Elastolin—Hitler in a civilian raincoat, Rudolf Hess in party uniform, Air-marshal Goering, a 'Blackshirt' and Hitler in the brown uniform of the S.A. ('Brownshirts'). The next figures are Lineol with Hindenburg and a general with a Spanish order. Franco is an Elastolin figure with a moveable saluting arm. Mussolini is a Lineol figure as is General Mackensen in his hussar uniform.

Plate 27

The early Britains' cavalry as a Victorian-style toy soon changed to a more anatomically accurate horse. The Life Guards officer in the middle appeared in box no. 1 of 1893. The cast-in tinplate sword also appeared on the improved Life Guard trooper of 1899. Early boxes also contained horsemen covered in gilt paint, a process which has preserved them well. The Blues trooper on the right was also from the first mould and appeared in box no. 2. The prancing hussar officer was in boxes 21 and 13. The Irish Lancers appeared in box 23 of 1894. The trooper had a fixed lance arm and the sideways-sitting officer was based on the *Army and Navy Gazette* plate of March 1889 by R. Simkin. This Scots Grey trooper first appeared in box 32 of 1895 and has a fixed tin sword.

Plate 28

The first Household-Cavalry-band figures had slotted arms but the moveable arms came in 1911. The Life-Guards officer and troopers are of the improved types of 1902 and 1913 respectively. The trumpeter and the farrier with his axe came out in 1954. These are all Britains' figures.

Plate 29

This collection of hussars include some repainted Britains' figures. The 11th-Hussars officer on the prancing horse is the improved model of 1909 but the hussars are of an earlier model. The 13th Hussars (with white busby bag) by 1903 had the same horse for both officer and man. The unique dismounted party of four men and four horses of the 11th Hussars appeared in 1913. The figures here have been repainted as the 4th and 19th Hussars. The dismounted bandsman of the 3rd Hussars is converted from an R.A.F. bandsman.

Plate 30

Britains produced many lancer types. The sideways-sitting officer has appeared previously but is here represented as one of the 16th Lancers. The lancers behind are of the standard popular figure, the same figure being painted as a 5th Lancer officer. Those on the left in white tropical helmets are of the 17th Lancers in white plastrons and of the 21st Lancers with blue-grey plastrons which came out some time after the battle of Omdurman, 1898. The 21st Lancers appeared in full dress the following year in box 100, the horse being a new, trotting type. The marching bandsman was converted in the thirties when massed bands at tattoos made a special appeal to the collectors.

Plate 31

The firm of Britains did not restrict its production to British soldiers but readily produced soldiers in conflicts overseas. Boer cavalry was in box no. 6. These fixed-arm troopers wore black hats, the convention of the period to distinguish the Boer. The Boer infantry appeared in box no. 26, also in black hats. The raid made by Dr. Jameson on the Boers in 1896 was popularized in box no. 38 in which the S. A. Mounted Infantry appeared. These were Boer cavalry painted differently, the Doctor having a blue collar. The infantry at the trail are Dublin Fusiliers of 1901. The slouch-hatted infantryman 'at the charge' is a City Imperial Volunteer of 1900 with an oval stand. The officer is a later improvement of 1907. The Scotsman in the white foreign service helmet is a Cameron Highlander.

Plate 32

Picturesque Highlanders were introduced by Britains in 1893, box 11 being running men of the Black Watch with plugged-in right arms. This figure changed in 1903 to the charging Highlander still on an oval stand. The marching Highlander appeared in 1901 and had the same base. Simplified equipment was given to the 1911 figure. The Cameron Highlander is from the 'A' series. The heavy standing Highlander with rifle at the trail is a B.M.C. figure. The white-helmeted firing figures are Britains' but those at the back are 'penny' figures of unknown make.

Plate 33

The Royal Welsh Fusiliers appeared in Britains' box 74 and originally had full equipment and gaiters. Britains' goat mascot had no goat-major and the one depicted here is by J. Hill Co. The band is from repainted soldiers.

Plate 34

The Royal Horse Artillery team in review order came out of Britains' box 39 in 1895. The horses were galloping and had an officer as appears on the left. The two seated gunners were later replaced by four mounted men. After the First World War box 316 had the Royal Horse Artillery with standing horses. The gun and limber have been altered in the group photographed. The standing officer at the back is a Carman figure made after the Second World War.

Plate 35

The Royal Field Artillery gun team appeared in 1906 (Britains' box 144) with horses at the walk. Two men were seated on the limber and two on the gun which had removable seats. The first horses had heavy collar harnesses but after the First World War this was changed to the simple harness as seen in the picture. Khaki versions of the team were produced. The original officer on the walking horse may be seen on the left. Box 317 was also in review order but with standing horses. On the right are the Royal Marine Artillery men in packs, one on the old oval stand. The marching gunners at the back are repaints but the standing officer in front is a Carman figure.

Plate 36

The mountain artillery came out in 1895 as Britains' box 28. The first mules have bent legs and are slightly smaller than the next versions which have straighter legs. Three mules carry the pieces of the gun which fix together and fire the ammunition carried on the fourth mule. The first mounted officer is at the head of the column but in 1910 his horse changed to a straight-legged type. Originally the six walking gunners were smaller and on oval stands. Shown in the picture are the later version on rectangular stands.

Plate 37

Britains produced an elaborate pontoon wagon soon after the First World War. The folding wooden sections opened up to make a bridge over the pontoon (also of wood). The four horses originally had collar harnesses but soon changed to the simplified equipment. The additional staff seen here have been converted from other Britains' figures, the busby having been re-introduced in 1936.

Plate 38

Britains do not seem to have issued box 137 for the Medical Services until 1904 although several of the 24 figures were based on a Simkin plate of March 1897. The two officers and the nurse were taken from this picture. The ambulance (no. 145) came out in 1906 and had a folding cloth cover. Although most of the personnel were in Army Service Corps uniform one seated man is (correctly) in the Medical Corps dress.

Plate 39

Britains issued the wagon of the Army Service Corps (no. 146) at the same time as the ambulance but the limbered wagon did not appear until 1934 as no. 1329. The other three figures are repainted from other Britains' figures.

Plate 40

The Royal Navy could not be overlooked by a British manufacturer. Both Bluejackets and Whitejackets appeared in 1898. These running figures had a rifle at the trail for the former and at the slope for the latter. The landing party with gun and limber came out at the same time with eight men holding the ropes. The gun was that of the mountain artillery battery. The standing seaman at the 'shoulder arms' for the Royal Naval Reserve was brought out in 1907 but the standing officer did not appear until the early thirties when the marching midshipman and the cocked-hat officers also came out in the same box. Straw-hatted sailors were sold as single 'A' figures but box 1510 produced marching sailors with moveable right arm and bell-bottomed trousers. The diver and the lifeguard are from Taylor and Barrett as is the standing guard with the diamond stands.

Plate 41

The early Royal Marine Artillery men of 1895 were given new heads in 1922 and became known as Royal Marines. It was not until about 1933 that the Royal Marines Band was introduced in two boxes of 21 and 12 men respectively. The marines following the band are the improved model without gaiters. At the back are four men of the plastic eyes-right series which was introduced when lead-casting was dying out. The high standard of modelling is noticeable.

Plate 42

It was not until 1925 that Britains produced box 240 for the Royal Air Force. There was an officer with a collar and tie and airmen with closed collars. Both wore puttees and have moveable left arms. In 1931 a monoplane with a pilot was produced. John Hill Company made the running pilot in white as well as the walking pilot and the mechanics. Taylor and Barrett were responsible for the guard of honour at the back. The Women's Royal Air Force is by Britains and was one of the figures in box 1894. The R.A.F. Regiment figures were made at the time of the 1953 coronation.

Plate 43

Messrs. Britains produced three boxes of Indian Cavalry as early as 1896. These included Skinner's Horse in bright yellow garments. Native infantry did not come until the next year. The bigger infantry figure came in 1911 and the Gurkhas in their dark green uniforms appeared during the First World War. The early infantry was revived in service dress as the Indian Army Service Corps at the beginning of the Second World War. The kneeling solid lead figure is a Mignot and the unpainted piper a Rose model by Russell Gamage. The khaki-clad Sikh with his legs apart is an Eriksson model made for Authenticast. Other figures are modifications of Britains' originals.

Plate 44

The African group is a very mixed bag. Britains brought out the first camels for the Egyptian Camel Corps in 1896 and the infantry arrived five years later. The large camel at the back for the 'Arabs of the Desert' came out during the First World War. The Arabs on foot appeared before the war but the running type

Plate 45

came after the Second World War. The seated Arabs and other standing types are of French manufacture in the 1930s. The Spahi on the horse and the North African in the large straw hat are pre-war Mignot figures. The camel kettle-drummer and other camel types are French solids destined for ornaments and ashtrays.

Plate 46

Cheap though Britains' soldiers may have been, an attempt was made to supply a cheaper market with 'B' and smaller 45 mm soldiers. Oval bases distinguish the early models, rectangular coming later. The early cavalry types had moving arms but later economies brought fixed arms. The infantry always had fixed arms.

Plate 47

Foreign soldiers were provided with Japanese, Russian and American types. The marching Belgian infantryman came as late as 1912. The Egyptian camel-rider was to be found in the 'A' series.

Plate 48

Britains at times emulated the large size Heyde figure but this range was limited to a few foot soldiers. The red-coated infantryman is '4h' and the Red Indian is in the same group. The first two figures are lifeboatmen of differing dates created for fund-raising. The Highlander on the extreme right is a 'Johillco' example of 60 mm

Plate 49

height. The remaining two are of American make, one a private (marked AM), 78 mm, of the American Revolutionary War period and the other a French soldier by an unknown commercial firm.

Plate 50

The introduction of plastic material after the Second World War permitted many countries to produce their own distinctive soldiers cheaply. The three figures on the left are gendarmes from Monaco. The next three in grey are Portuguese armed forces which include police. The next three can be nothing but Greek, the evzone brandishing his flag, the infantryman still wearing a shako but the modern commando in a netted steel helmet.

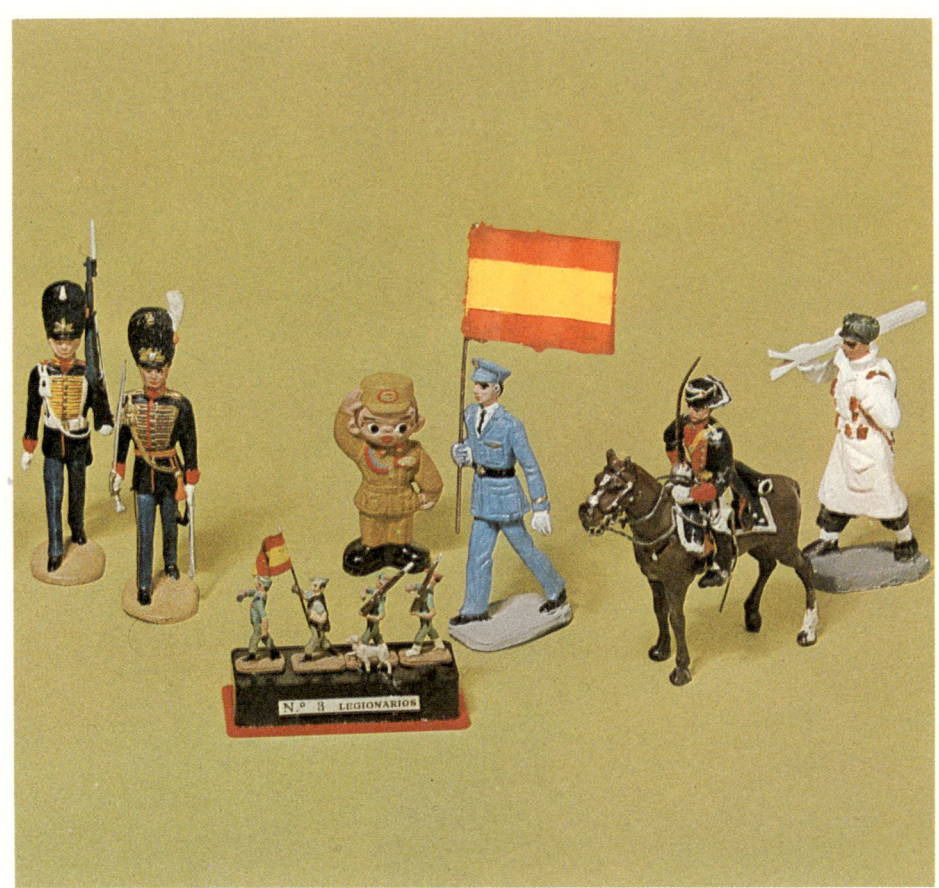

Plate 51

The two elegant Guardsmen are from the Netherlands. The remaining Spanish soldiers include a dumpy recruit made of clay, an elegant ensign with the Spanish flag (made of plastic) and the small Legionarios are made of lead. The very detailed cavalry piece with separate reins was made before the war in Barcelona. The ski-trooper is a modern plastic toy sold in the cheapest shops.

Plate 52

The expense of lead and the fragile nature of toys made in the hollow manner led to experiments with aluminium. The French firm of Mignalu in the thirties produced a popular toy but the material only allowed figures of poor definition. Storybook uniforms and even an officer on a rocking horse were on the market. The search for an overseas market brought Life Guards and Foot Guards. The firm of Wend-al Toys Ltd., of Blandford, sold many of these figures in England but they were not popular with the collectors. Since the war Soldalu in France continues to produce modern French soldiers. Germany had a range of aluminium and other alloy figures in the flat tradition but the range was never extensive despite the good finish and artistic detail.

Plate 53

Obviously the most artistic soldiers must be produced in the round or third dimension. Cast metal seemed to be the answer for the firm of Heyde in the nineteenth century. In Dresden they made solid soldiers in sizes ranging from 40 to 90 mm. The mounted figure of the Scots Grey is in the 90 mm scale. The mounted infantry officer in the 80 mm scale has a sword which can be withdrawn from its tinplate scabbard. His helmet is removable, as are those of the following infantrymen, who also have separate rifles and packs. The musicians (68 mm) have small fur head-dresses which betray their German origin, but the Foot Guardsman has a better bearskin. The naval officers are definitely German in character. The Highland Light Infantry soldier is in the 55 mm size and has an attached shoulder plaid.

Plate 54

The successful commercial rivalry of Messrs. Britains at the end of the nineteenth century reduced the sales of the expensive Heyde figures. The firm now concentrated on the smaller figure capable of permutations and alteration. Here the Foot Guards band has a variety of musical instruments soldered on to the pliable arms. The civilian types graced many a toy railway station and in fact appeared in photographs of H. G. Wells's *Floor Games*.

Plate 55

Just after the First World War Courtenay and Doran made hollow-cast figures of 45 mm scale depicting fighting men of the Middle Ages. These are the two figures on foot in the middle. R. Courtenay worked on his own to produce solid knights for which he became famous. He was the first British person to produce the connoisseur figure with its meticulous painting of heraldic arms. Men with moveable arms in the tradition of Britains were later changed to figures like those on the left which have arms and weapons which were soldered on.

Plate 56

Although Britains retailed a penny figure of a knight (based on the armour of Henry VIII) it was not until 1933 that they produced a Tournament of six pieces. Otto Gottstein, in about 1951, backed a project for hollow-cast medieval knights. When Gottstein died the moulds were taken over by Messrs. Britain as the Knights of Agincourt. These most elaborate figures do not accurately portray the dress of contemporary figures. When plastic 'swoppets' came on to the market the medieval figures continued the flamboyant fashion although not strictly accurate in costume or armour.

Plate 57

Until recently other historical periods were not produced commercially. Saxon and Norman figures were made after the Second World War in a limited edition. The Magna Carta knights were made with interchangeable heads and weapons and sold in Burlington Arcade and Regent Street, London. The civilian figures were also produced by Carman soon after the 1939–45 war but are individually modelled.

Plate 58

Courtenay made certain royal personages in the late thirties, like Charles I in this group of Royalists. To fill a commercial gap the pikemen and musketeers were produced just before the 1939 war by Carman. The range was extended by the addition of officers, cavalry and women, after the war. Other figures were specially produced from plaster moulds. Today the flexible mould has extended the possibilities of detail and reduced the basic work of producing new figures. The old metal moulds are now of historical interest.

Plate 59

In the nineteen-thirties Holger Eriksson in Sweden carved horses from wood for his own enjoyment. He gradually developed a technique and output which has spread all round the world. The standing Roman with the attached shield may have been his first metal figure. The elegant 17th Lancers figures show his careful modelling of horses. The marching soldiers on the left were made for Authenticast and an Irish company while the small 30 mm figures in the centre were produced by the Swedish African Engineers (S.A.E.), when the business moved to South Africa. Holger Eriksson now makes and retails his soldiers from Sweden, still keeping a high standard of finish.

Plate 60

Before 1939 certain American manufacturers made hollow-cast Revolutionary War soldiers like the two on the left. At the same time, in France, Auger made a solid standard bearer from a metal mould, but the outbreak of the war limited the extension of this market. After the war Madame Metayer marketed many French and some British soldiers of the Napoleonic period, said to have been designed by L. Rousselot. The second man on the right, an infantryman c. 1804 is one of these. The flamboyant hussar in his tall watering cap is from Graham Farish, which firm made oversize solid figures from flexible moulds at the time of the 1953 coronation. The blue light dragoon, third from left, is from the Stadden miniature firm, and is a solid figure from a flexible mould, and setting the trend for the many military miniatures of today. The maid, based on a Sandby water-colour and on Mary Ann Todd dressed as a drummer finding her dead officer-lover, are pre-1939 solid figures cast by W. Y. Carman.

Plate 61

The 54 mm solid figures here depict the French of Napoleon's time. Somewhere in the nineteenth century Lucotte of Paris began these characteristic solid soldiers made in metal moulds, with plug-in heads, attached arms and separate furniture for the horses. The five cavalry figures are all on the 'ploughing-through-the-snow', horse. The infantry had rectangular stands frequently embossed with the 'Imperial Bee' of Napoleon Buonaparte. These continued to be made even in modern times but always retaining their antique appearance. The new figures produced by Madame Metayer—the grenadier on the extreme right—shows the vast improvement of an artist-designed soldier. Napoleon and the *cantinière* are solid figures made by Carman just after the Second World War.

Plate 62

To balance the 'Mond' collection of French soldiers in the Royal United Services Museum, the British Model Soldier Society began making models of the British at Waterloo. To aid this endeavour Britains produced an infantryman and a Highlander. Conversions of the latter may be seen at the back of the plate, on the left. The Royal Horse Guard and the Scots Grey are early Eriksson figures. The mounted Horse Artillery officer is a converted Britain figure. The fusilier officer waving his sword is a Stadden. The remainder are Carman soldiers, the marching infantryman coming out before the war, but the rifleman, light infantry and Becky Sharp appeared in the late forties.

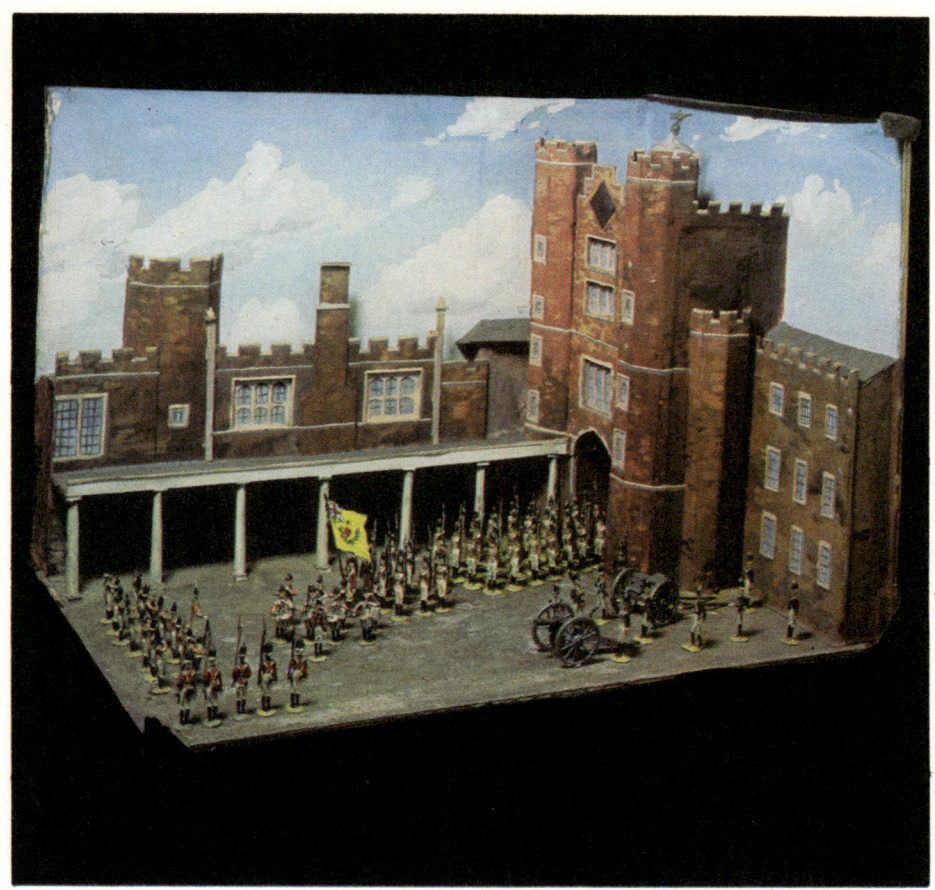

Plate 63

The attraction of the one inch or 30 mm figures, in the solid, led to the making of the set of soldiers of 1800, in two-piece slate moulds in 1938, a pattern to be followed later by Greenwood and others.

The model of Colour Court in St. James's Palace has an artillery gun team which may never have been seen in that august place normally reserved for the Foot Guards, since it is the place where the colours lodged during guard-mounting.

Plate 64

During the Second World War Greenwood changed from his 40 mm medieval figures to the 25-30 mm scale. He produced the basic figure by sand-casting, and animated the figures with delicate soldering like the string on the bow of the Egyptian archer. His animation of Wellingtonian groups was very lively and the careful painting of Miss Ball brought a wide market to their product.

The figures on the left by Colonel J. B. R. Nicholson are trial soldiers, made later when flexible moulds were available, and seem to be inspired by the Siborne warriors. The 20 mm English-Civil-War soldiers on the right are by J. Niblett and may still be purchased in the West End of London.

photograph: P. O. Stearns

Plate 65

Edward Suren, maker of 'Willie' 30 mm figures, began modelling as a hobby, but soon found that his figures were sought after. The setting of this picture is Rorke's Drift in the Zulu War 1879, site of a heroic action. The attacking Zulus have climbed over the barricades of boxes and are attacking the men of the 24th South Wales Borderers. The makeshift hospital is to be seen at the back of the verandah. The face of each soldier has its own character despite the fact that the figure is only an inch high.

SELECT BIBLIOGRAPHY

BLUM, Peter, *Military Miniatures*, Hamlyn, London, 1964; Golden Press, New York, 1964
BOESGAARD, N. E., *Tinge-linge-later tinsoldater*, Thejls, 1967
GARRATT, John, G., *Model Soldiers*, Seeley Service, London, 1959
HAMPE, T., *Der Zinnsoldat*, Stubenrauch, 1924
HARRIS, Henry, *Model Soldiers*, Weidenfeld and Nicolson, London, 1962; Putnam's, New York, 1962
MARTIN, P., *Der Standhafte Zinnsoldat*, Franckh, 1961; *Les Petits Soldats de Strasbourg*, Compagnie des Arts Photomécaniques, 1950
MARTIN, P. & VAILLANT, M., *Le Monde Merveilleux*, Massin, 1960
RICHARDS, L. W., *Old British Model Soldiers, 1893–1918*, Arms & Armour Press, London, 1970; Tricorn, New York, 1970
RISLEY, C. A. & IMRIE, W. F., *Model Soldier Guide*, Risley and Imrie, New York, 1965
WELLS, H. G., *Floor Games*, F. Palmer, London, 1911; *Little Wars*, F. Palmer, London, 1913, facsimile edition, Arms & Armour Press, London, 1970; Macmillan, New York, 1970

SELECTED MUSEUMS WHERE DISPLAYS MAY BE SEEN

FRANCE: Historical Museum, Strasbourg; Miniature Figurines Museum, Compiègne; Musée de L'Armee, Paris
GERMANY: Bayerisches Museum, Munich; Germanisches Museum, Nuremberg; Tin Figure Museum, Plassenburg Castle, Kulmbach
SPAIN: Army Museum, Madrid
SWITZERLAND: Landesmuseum, Zurich
UNITED KINGDOM: Bethnal Green Museum, London; Blenheim Palace, Oxfordshire; London Museum, London; Museum of Childhood, Edinburgh; Oaklands Park Museum, Chelmsford; Royal Tunbridge Wells Museum, Tunbridge Wells; Wilton House, Salisbury
U.S.A.: Heritage Plantation, Sandwich, Massachusetts; West Point Museum, United States Military Academy, West Point, New York
U.S.S.R.: Artillery Museum, Leningrad